Original title:
Rose Reflections

Copyright © 2025 Creative Arts Management OÜ
All rights reserved.

Author: Nash Everly
ISBN HARDBACK: 978-1-80567-020-9
ISBN PAPERBACK: 978-1-80567-100-8

The Essence of Forgotten Gardens

In the garden where veggies grow,
The flowers argue, putting on a show.
The carrots dance, the peas take flight,
While weeds just giggle all through the night.

A sunflower wears a floppy hat,
Pretends to be a cool, old cat.
The daisies whisper, share some glee,
While twirling 'round a bumblebee.

The tomatoes squash their stage fright,
And start to sing, oh what a sight!
But lettuce rolls its sleepy eyes,
And moans for more garden pies.

A cabbage tells a joke so green,
Even the squashes shine and preen.
In this patch, laughter's always free,
While fickle blooms sip herbal tea.

Whispered Secrets of the Bloom

In the garden, petals sigh,
Bees wearing tiny bowties fly.
Flowers gossip of their dreams,
Like comedians in sunbeam schemes.

Tulips trade their fashion tips,
While daisies practice funny quips.
Lilies blush and giggle bright,
In the soft embrace of night.

A Crescendo of Floral Thoughts

Daisies debate the best mascara,
While violets write their own sonata.
Peonies dream of their starlit show,
With rhymes that only florals know.

Chrysanthemums plan a grand parade,
Twirling petals for a fresh upgrade.
Sunflowers grinning, tall and bold,
In this garden, laughter unfolds.

Blossoms in the Twilight

Evening blooms with a cheeky grin,
Chasing fireflies, they dance and spin.
Marigolds share the day's gossip loud,
As shadows mingle, feeling proud.

Pansies chuckle at the day's old news,
Winking petals in colorful hues.
All bloomers know how to unwind,
Beneath the stars, their fun combined.

The Dance of Blooming Shadows

Under the moon, petals sway with glee,
Waltzing shadows play hide and seek, you see.
A rose jokes, says, 'I'm just a thorny type!'
While blooms whisper, 'Let's create the hype!'

Jasmine twirls in the midnight air,
With marigolds singing without a care.
In every fragrance, laughter blooms,
In the garden, joy utterly consumes.

Harmonies of Petal and Time

In the garden where flowers dance,
A petal slipped, lost its chance.
It twirled away, in a leaf's embrace,
"Oh dear!" it cried, "What a funny place!"

The sunbeams laughed and cast their glow,
As bees tickled buds with a buzz and a flow.
Petals sang in a cheeky rhyme,
Together they bounced, defying time.

Petals in the Mirror

A blossom looked and giggled wide,
"Who's that staring? Oh, what a ride!"
With petals bright and colors bold,
It struck a pose, so young and old.

It twirled once more in a mirror's gaze,
"Is that my best side?" it asked in a haze.
A butterfly winked, full of glee,
"Just focus on fun; let your heart be free!"

Thorns and Dreams

In a field where thorns stood tall,
A dream floated, gave a call.
"Hey thorns, don't poke just stand in place,
Let's have a laugh, not a prickly race!"

They chuckled and tumbled, quite absurd,
A prickly party with one silly word.
"Dare to dream, don't be a bore,
We'll dance all night till we can't anymore!"

Truths Hidden in Soft Petals

In a garden of whispers, secrets play,
Soft petals flutter, chasing blues away.
Bumblebees gossip, oh what a treat,
While ants in tuxedos dance to the beat.

The sun wears sunglasses, sipping sweet tea,
It wonders aloud, what could this life be?
Petals conceal laughter, in a whimsical swirl,
Each fragrant giggle gives the world a twirl.

A spider's web glimmers, like dreams that ignite,
Promising fortune, but just on a kite.
The daisies chuckle, oh what a sight,
As they tumble and tumble, in pure delight.

Under the moonlight, all truths shall fade,
For petals know humor, in every charade.
With each gentle sway, their stories unfold,
In laughter and petals, all mysteries told.

A Tangle of Love and Distance

Two hearts on a wire, like cats in a tree,
Chasing after love, so utterly free.
Their branches get twisted, a messy affair,
While squirrels take bets on how they'll repair.

Each phone call an acrobat, soaring through air,
Words tumble like circus tricks, sprinkled with flair.
A wink from the distance, a grin that confounds,
Though miles apart, still teamed up in rounds.

The postman delivers with a roll of his eyes,
Love letters that giggle, wrapped up in disguise.
Beneath all the fuss, there's a beautiful dance,
These tangled hearts laugh, at their own silly chance.

With dreams made of giggles, they scatter and twist,
In tangles of love, they can't help but persist.
From far-away places, the laughter breaks through,
In the circus of romance, they both know what's true.

Blossoms Beneath the Still Waters

In ponds of reflection, the lily pads grin,
While frogs in tuxedos declare they'll win.
Each splash tells a tale of love that's afloat,
As water nymphs gossip from their dreamboat.

The goldfish do pirouettes, proud of their flair,
While ducks on a mission convene to compare.
Amid twirls of color, both vibrant and bold,
The blossoms are laughing secrets untold.

Ripples roll gently, like whispers so sly,
Each petal's a joke, that simply won't die.
Beneath all the calm, there's a giggle so sweet,
In nature's own pause, the antics repeat.

With the moon as their witness, they plot and they scheme,
In waters of laughter, they float like a dream.
Each blossom a story, so funny and bright,
Reflecting pure joy in the stillness of night.

Echoing Beauty in Layers

In layers of laughter, the petals reside,
Each outermost layer holds stories that hide.
As bumblebees buzz, and butterflies flutter,
They giggle at truths that make sweetness mutter.

From blushing pink blush to vibrant wild yellows,
Each color a secret, shared by the fellows.
In layers of chaos, they twist and they twine,
Crafting arrangements that seem so divine.

Underneath veils of fragrance, jokes softly bloom,
With every sweet whiff, they lighten the gloom.
Petals in laughter, unfurl with a wink,
Their humor a dance, making flowers rethink.

So toast to the beauty, the layers we wear,
In blooms of pure joy, let's give love a dare.
In echoing laughter, we sparkle and sway,
For the heart of the garden, is funny today.

Scented Memories of Youth

In gardens where we played all day,
With sticky fingers, we'd laugh and sway.
Petals in our hair, what a sight!
We'd spin in circles, oh what delight!

Once spilled juice on a picnic spread,
Got chased by bees, oh the dread!
Mom yelled, 'Don't eat that, it's not a treat!'
But we just wanted more sugary sweets!

Under the sun, we raced and ran,
Dared each other, 'Can you catch this can?'
Scent of flowers, a childish whim,
But oh, that day really went dim!

We grew up fast, but what a phase,
Still chase those scents through life's maze.
With laughter left in every breeze,
Here's to youth, and memories that tease!

A Garden of Echoing Souls

In the garden where we'd play hide and seek,
A bee buzzed loud, and we felt weak!
'Is that a bug or just our fears?'
Laughter rang out, drowning our tears.

Flowers chatting with gossiping glee,
'Did you hear what they said about me?'
Tulips blush, while daisies cheer,
In this botanical drama, we disappear!

We'd plant our dreams in the soil so deep,
Water them with giggles, and secrets to keep.
And if the weeds dared to come and creep,
We'd rally our forces, wake from our sleep!

Yet, time marches on, the blooms start to fade,
But those echoes of laughter never evade.
In every petal, every sprout,
Childhood whispers still dance about!

Crimson Shades Beneath the Moon

Under the moon, we make our camp,
Filled with giggles and a wilted lamp.
'Let's catch the stars!' someone would yell,
As we tumbled down, oh what a spell!

Playing tag with shadows, a mischievous game,
The moonlight laughing, calling our name.
But ouch! That thorn caught my toe!
'Well, that's what you get for moving too slow!'

In deep crimson colors, we drew our plans,
Sipping juice from our funny cans.
With every hiccup, the laughter would soar,
As we made silly jokes, begging for more!

But deep in those hues, memories gleamed,
As we whispered hopes, with giggles we dreamed.
Each midnight adventure, a story to tell,
Even with thorns, we loved it so well!

The Language of Thorned Serendipity

In the garden of mishaps, we learned to peruse,
Each thorny embrace taught us not to lose.
With snickers and giggles, we ventured ahead,
Crashing through bushes, but never in dread!

'Watch where you step!' a wise voice crooned,
But who needed caution when mischief loomed?
In a tangle of laughter, we'd tumble and trip,
'Just pat my back, take a chance on this flip!'

Memories piled like leaves in the fall,
Thorny tales laughed, tender yet tall.
With every bruise, a badge of our youth,
We'd trade scars for stories, seeking the truth.

So here's to the blooms with edges so sharp,
They taught us the rhythm of life's playful harp.
In the garden of misfits, we'll twirl and spin,
For amidst all the thorns, our joy will always win!

Fragrant Echoes of the Heart

In a garden so spry and merry,
Petals tickle bees that are hairy.
They dance in the air, quite a sight,
Buzzing tunes that feel just right.

The thorns seem to wear a frown,
While petals giggle, spinning around.
A bouquet with secrets to share,
Plucking laughter from fragrant air.

Butterflies wear hats and twirl,
Whispering jokes as they whirl.
But the gardener just rolls his eyes,
"Not again!" he sighs with surprise.

Yet every bloom has a tale to spin,
Of mischief where the fun begins.
In the realm of colors bright and bold,
Laughter is worth its weight in gold.

Tapestry of Blossom and Thought

In fields where colors laugh and play,
Buds confetti the light of day.
Petals plush on a velvet breeze,
Dancing like kids with wobbly knees.

A daisy whispers to a fern,
"Let's scheme a plan for a twisty turn!"
While daisies boast of their sunny charm,
A tulip snickers, "I raise the alarm!"

Marigolds poke fun at all who pass,
"Hey, stop and smell us, we're first-class!"
While violets giggle, soft and coy,
"Let's bloom big and bring some joy!"

And somewhere deep in nature's art,
Laughter prances, its own sweet heart.
Together, each bloom finds its play,
In the garden where fun leads the way.

Shattered Petals, Silent Songs

A petal slips from a budding friend,
"Oops!" it cries, "This isn't the end!"
It lands in a puddle with a splash,
And chuckles to itself with a dash.

In silent songs, petals ponder,
About the bees that buzz and wander.
"Did they forget to wear their hats?"
"Or did the fungus chat with bats?"

Bursting laughter like morning sun,
Buds reveal their singular fun.
A dandelion giggles at its fate,
"I'm the weed, but aren't I great?"

As petals drift on a gentle breeze,
They whisper softly between the trees.
In petals' truth, the silly sings,
Life is funny; oh, what joy it brings!

The Mirror's Blooming Secrets

In a pond where reflections meet,
Blooms gossip with petals, quite the feat!
Leaves wink at their own fair face,
"Do I look good in this sunny place?"

A flower preens in a water's glance,
"Do I get extra points for my dance?"
While the canary bursts into song,
"Your mirror is where you belong!"

The tulip speaks with a flair so grand,
"I'm the fairest in this land!"
But lilacs trail after with a chuckle,
"Keep talking, dear; you're merely a snuggle!"

And petals converse with great delight,
In the mirror's truth amidst the light.
Their secrets bloom, as laughter spills,
In a garden bright with joyous thrills.

The Language of Withering

In the garden, whispers grow,
Petals gossip, soft and slow.
Colors fade, yet jokes remain,
A thorny grin hides the pain.

Leaves giggle in the breeze,
Dancing under bumblebee tease.
From vibrant hues to faded brown,
Still they wear the silliest frown.

When morning dew spills secrets low,
Sunlight's laughter starts to glow.
With every shade that starts to part,
A punchline tickles the old heart.

So here's a toast to blooms that jest,
Though beauty fades, they still invest.
In the soil of unfunny days,
They share their humor in wild ways.

Secrets Between the Stems

In the patch where petals laugh,
Secrets bloom like a silly gaffe.
Stems conspire when no one's near,
Whispering softly, 'Did you hear?'

Buzzing bees with puns on wings,
Tickling tulips with funny things.
In nature's playbook, jokes unfold,
Stories told in colors bold.

Underneath the sunlit chat,
Cacti chuckle at the chitchat.
Laughter breaks like morning dew,
While daisies plot their next debut.

With every poke and prickly tease,
They sway and giggle in the breeze.
So let's enjoy this garden cheer,
Where every bloom has humor near.

Petal-Silence in the Twilight

In the twilight, petals lie low,
Hushed giggles through shadows flow.
As night approaches, jokes conceal,
Mirth in silence, a playful feel.

Stars peek in with an eager grin,
Wondering where the fun begins.
A bloom leans close, with secrets told,
Of how the moonlight makes them bold.

Crickets chirp their nightly tune,
While blossoms wear their dreamy swoon.
In moonlit silence, soft and light,
They chuckle softly, what a sight!

As night wraps all in velvet airs,
Each petal's stories danced in pairs.
So when the dawn begins to break,
Laughter stirs awake, make no mistake!

The Briefest Burst of Color

In a blink, they burst alive,
Colors flashing, oh, how they thrive!
A moment's dance, then fading fast,
Chasing giggles, in summer's blast.

Sunshine's winks, a playful tease,
Becomes a bloom of sheer unease.
Tickled petals wave goodbye,
As flitting hues begin to fly.

With each quick laugh at nature's play,
Every petal finds its way.
Yet in their haste, they spark delight,
In fleeting bursts, they steal the night.

So let us cherish blooms so bright,
With laughter wrapped in morning light.
For every pop that graces eyes,
Is just a joke in nature's guise.

Mosaic of Nature's Palette

Amidst petals of pink and yellow,
A butterfly wears socks, quite the fellow.
He dances with bees in the midday sun,
Claiming all nectar, thinking it's fun.

In gardens so lush, the critters debate,
Who smells the best on this glorious date.
The daisies giggle, the tulips just pout,
While the daisies proclaim, "We're the talk of the route!"

A squirrel in shades, lounging in style,
Counts blossoms like coins, with a cheeky smile.
"One for the pals, and one for my nest,
These blooms are my currency; I'm truly blessed!"

Every petal a canvas, colors galore,
Nature's giggles echo, we simply adore.
With each silly stem and each playful sprout,
The patchwork of life is what it's all about!

Traces of Blooming Melancholy

In the garden of glee, a sunflower frowns,
He's tired of wearing those heavyweight crowns.
While the others all sway, singing with cheer,
He's plotting revenge on the neighbor's deer.

A daffodil's joke takes a twist on a whim,
"Why don't we bloom on the edge of the brim?"
The roses all giggle, the violets chime,
"All's fair in love, and we're ahead of the time!"

The wind tells tall tales of blooms from the past,
Of blossoms that rivaled the great ones so vast.
But the petals just shrug, "Oh, it's all in good fun,
We'll bloom in our style and still be number one!"

With shadows that dance, and laughter that sings,
Even weeds find a way to flaunt their own flings.
In a patchwork of giggles and memories that swell,
Each blossom a story, in their floral carousel.

A Symphony of Thorn and Silk

Oh, the big prickly bushes gossip with flair,
While smooth silk petals swish with great care.
"Did you hear what the thorns said at noon?
They think they can win the thorny balloon!"

In the choir of petals, a trumpet does blare,
"Watch out for bugs with their lightweight affair!"
The petals all blush, while the bark starts to snicker,
"A leaf in the breeze is the ultimate kicker!"

The daisies demonstrate their funky new stance,
While the vines do their dance, it's a wild romance.
Thorns shout encouragement as blooms take the lead,
This funny ensemble's the garden's own creed!

So they sway and they twist, a playful ballet,
Nature's big joke on a sunny ballet.
In each thriving garden, the laughter's our song,
A symphony playing where all of us belong!

Illusions of Floral Grace

In a battlefield of blooms, a daisy will shout,
"Watch me twirl, just see what I'm about!"
While tulips roll their eyes at the foe,
"Your dance looks more like a sneeze or a throw!"

With petals so bright and leaves that are spry,
A buttercup boasts, "I can touch the sky!"
But a stubborn old fern, with a grin on his face,
Whispers, "Not with that wobble, you'll land with disgrace!"

The pansies declare it's a fashion faux pas,
And call for a meeting, "Let's applaud with a ha!"
In ribbons and ruffles, they prance to the beat,
While the violets giggle, just tapping their feet.

So amidst the confusion of colors and cheer,
Each flower is laughing, let's give them a cheer!
With hugs from the pollen and laughter like lace,
Nature's own comedy unfolds with such grace!

A Garden's Silent Secrets

In the garden blooms a sight,
Petals giggle in the light.
Whispers float on gentle breeze,
Plants gossip while you're at ease.

Bumblebees dance with no care,
Wearing pollen like a flare.
Tulips wink and daisies chuckle,
Nature's humor, a gentle shuffle.

Snails wear shells like tiny hats,
While frogs croon to charmed alley cats.
Laughter hides in every nook,
In the garden's playful book.

So when you take a stroll real slow,
Listen close, it's sure to show.
Beneath the blooms, a fun brigade,
Secret giggles serenade.

Blossoms Beneath the Stars

Under stars that gently sway,
Flowers plan a wild ballet.
Daisies twirl in moonlit glow,
Joking how they steal the show.

Nighttime comes with silly dreams,
Petals laugh in silver beams.
Crickets play their nightly tunes,
As blooms dance with overgrown spoons.

Beneath the moon's soft, cheeky light,
Cacti claim they're just as bright.
Mimicking stars, they puff with pride,
While nearby blooms just laugh and hide.

In this world of night-time cheer,
Flora's fun is crystal clear.
Join the blossoms in their play,
And laugh the sleepy night away.

The Essence of Velvet Hues

Softly blush in velvet sways,
Colors joke in subtle ways.
Crimson lines and lilac bends,
Each petal knows, they're all good friends.

Cheeky greens hide 'neath the blue,
Sprouting jokes that tickle you.
Amber yellows burst with glee,
Telling secrets only they see.

In the garden's vibrant grace,
Giggles bloom in every space.
Velvet hues with their sly smiles,
Compete for laughs, across the miles.

So take a moment, pause for fun,
Join the laughter, one by one.
In shades of soft and colors bright,
Find the joy that blooms each night.

Reflections in a Dew-Kissed Dawn

Morning breaks with wet delight,
Dewdrops dance in warm sunlight.
Pansies laugh with open eyes,
As sunlight paints the giant skies.

Glancing at reflections bright,
Every bloom becomes a sight.
Nature's mirror shows them grinning,
In this dawn, the fun's just beginning.

Petals sway with morning cheer,
Whispering jokes that we can hear.
Life wakes up in giggly tunes,
Underneath the shining moons.

So frolic through the dew-kissed morn,
With laughter's warmth, you'll be reborn.
For in each drop that sparkles wide,
Lie the smiles that will abide.

Secrets of the Blooming Heart

In a garden, secrets dwell,
Where petals whisper, oh so well.
A daisy giggles, a tulip snorts,
In this blooming land, they hold court!

Bees buzzing with gossip so sweet,
Sharing tales of pollen and beet.
They laugh at the roses, all dressed in flair,
While daisies just sit with their wild, crazy hair.

A sunflower spouts, 'I'm the tallest here!'
But a little wildflower yells, "Bring me a beer!"
They trade silly jokes in the dusky light,
As the garden bursts forth in delight!

So if you wander through blooms so fine,
Know that they're jesters, sipping on wine.
Laughter and colors blend in the air,
In the secrets of hearts that bloom without care.

Fragrance Beneath the Last Light

Under the soft glow of evening's stay,
Flowers are plotting their grand cabaret.
Petal dancers twirl in open glee,
While a daffodil shouts, 'Come dance with me!'

The wind teases with a fragrant splurge,
As marigolds laugh, they're ready to purge.
Stumbling and tumbling, they frolic around,
Till a frog joins in, leaping bound for bound!

Jasmine giggles as twilight draws near,
Spreading her scent like a wild frontier.
"Who knew we'd party beneath the last light?"
As blooms burst forth in jubilant flight!

So if you hear laughter in the dark,
Know that they're ready to make their mark.
For scents of the night with humor entwine,
Beneath the last light where petals align!

Echoing Blossoms of Grace

In a field where wild blooms chatter and cheer,
A daisy declares, "I'm the flower of the year!"
The violets snicker, "Oh, listen to her!"
As they wave their heads in a flowerful blur.

Up in the trees, a mockingbird laughs,
Singing of blossoms with silly gaffes.
"Petals like skirts, you bloomers in play,
Who knew floral life was this fun every day?"

But under the clover, a rogue weed plots,
To crash the party with awkward knots.
"Oh, I'm misunderstood, it's quite a disgrace!"
And yet all the flowers embraced him with grace.

So join in the laughter where petals unite,
In echoing blossoms that sparkle with light.
For in every crack and colorful hue,
There's humor and joy when the blooms break through!

Shadows of Floral Serenity

In the garden's shade, where secrets reside,
Petals conspire, there's nowhere to hide.
Carnations gossip with witty retorts,
While lurking behind, the shy pansy snorts.

"Hey, did you hear what the lilacs just said?"
Echoes of laughter as they roll in their bed.
The sunflowers nod, with faces so bright,
"Tickle me, darling, it's a floral delight!"

A breeze sweeps in with a rascally grin,
Swirling around as the petals all spin.
Dandelions puff, and they scatter their laughs,
While the roses roll eyes at their silly gaffes.

So wander through shadows where humor does bloom,
Find joy in the whispers of perfumed room.
For in floral serenity, laughter takes flight,
And blooms in the garden dance through the night!

The Heart Beneath the Petal

In a garden of laughter, blooms grow tall,
Whispers of flowers, with giggles, they call.
A dainty one sneezes, pollen in flight,
Paints the bees yellow, oh what a sight!

Thorns wear tiny hats, oh what a show,
Dancing in outfits, their best to bestow.
With petals like skirts, they twirl with glee,
Making us chuckle, a grand jubilee!

The sun plays peek-a-boo, making them blush,
As daisies tell secrets, in a light-hearted hush.
Bees buzzing like laughter, on nectar they dine,
In this floral circus, all's simply divine!

So let's join this waltz in the fragrant space,
Where whimsy and humor wear nature's grace.
In this garden of joy, no frown can persist,
For gobbling up laughter is how we exist!

Visions of a Forgotten Garden

In a garden forgotten, where giggles are sparse,
The weeds wear monocles and dance with a farce.
The statues are gossiping, with moss for a wig,
Telling tales of sunflowers who think they are big!

A snail in a top hat, quite proud of his pace,
Claims he's the fastest to win any race.
But frogs keep on laughing, their croaks full of jest,
'It's all in the timing!' they claim, unimpressed.

Lark's a jester, perched on a branch so high,
Making jokes about clouds that just drift by.
The daisies roll over, their petals in stitches,
Sure beats the talking and grumpiness bitches!

So skip to this garden, where joy's evergreen,
In the veil of the laughter, lies magic unseen.
For wisdom of blooms is that laughter's the key,
In this quirky old haven, come enjoy, come see!

Beyond the Silken Veil

Behind every petal, there's nonsense in bloom,
With gossiping leaves all dancing in gloom.
The silk ribbons swish, as the breeze tells a tale,
Of squirrels with acorns who dance without fail!

The roses throw parties, all petals and fluff,
But tulips are waiting, they've had quite enough!
They pout in their colors, a rainbow brigade,
While daisies are laughing, a sunny charade.

With laughter as fragrant as honey from hives,
The garden's alive, in its funny jives.
Bees play the drums, while butterflies sing,
In this world beneath, oh, the joy it can bring!

So peek through the veil, let the whimsy unfurl,
In the dance of the blooms, find a giggly swirl.
The laughter is endless, a riot of cheer,
In this magical garden, you'll shed every fear!

A Canvas of Inflorescence

In a canvas of colors, so bright and so loud,
Flowers wear costumes, they're fierce, they're proud.
The violets debate, who's the fairest of all,
While peonies blush, feeling tiny and small.

With laughter like petals that float in the breeze,
Each bloom has a story that tickles and teases.
The orchids, so regal, wear crowns made of dew,
As the sun sets the stage for the night's big debut!

A jolly old bumblebee, buzzing with cheer,
Claims he's the star, which everyone hears.
With the daisies as backup, they croon through the night,
In this show of inflorescence, oh what a sight!

So join in the merriment, let laughter unfold,
In the paintbrush of nature, let stories be told.
For life's just a garden, a whimsical spree,
Where humor and petals are wild and so free!

Echoes of Crimson Beauty

In a garden where petals play,
A squirrel stole flowers, in broad day.
With a wig and a strut, quite bold,
He thought he looked handsome, truth be told.

Bees buzzing round, dancing with glee,
Mistaking a hat for a new bumblebee.
They chase it about, up and then down,
While the squirrel just prances all over town.

A chubby gardener, grumbling away,
Complains of the antics that spoil his day.
"Those blooms were for beauty, not for this play!"
But who can resist a furry ballet?

So here's to the fools in the flower beds,
Inhabiting dreams and vying for heads.
In crimson and laughter, we find delight,
As petals and giggles take flight tonight.

Garden Whispers at Dusk

At twilight, the daisies start to gossip,
"Did you see how that tulip did flip?"
With petals aflutter, they share their tales,
Of a bumblebee's dance and tangled trails.

A dandelion, proud with a fluffy crown,
Claims he could win a floral renown.
"Watch me now, I'll blow and I'll fly!
Make sure you catch me before I say bye!"

The lilacs all snicker, they think it's a joke,
"Last time you did that, you turned into smoke!"
And the violets giggle, oh what a sight,
As the garden erupts into laughter tonight.

So when the sun sets and shadows presume,
Join in the fun of this floral costume.
Listen closely to flowers in chat,
As the echoes of laughter linger at that.

Velvet Hues of Memory

A velvet petal, soft as a sigh,
Is convinced it's the star of the butterfly fly.
"Look at me dance in this marvelous beam!"
While the others just chuckle, suppressing a scream.

"Your color's divine, it's no contest!"
Said a daisy, dressed up in her Sunday best.
"We know you're the finest, but keep it down,
You're making the tulips just tremble and frown."

The daisies hold court, in their squeaky tone,
Pronouncing themselves as shades of gold.
But when the laughter fades and night claims its right,
The velvet petal winks, 'See you at night!'

In the moonlight's laugh, the blooms all conspire,
To dance and to prance, and create their own choir.
Underneath the stars, the garden's a beat,
Where memories bloom, and silliness meets.

Reflections on Soft Blossoms

In a mirror of dew, the petals preen,
Discussing their vitality, glossy and keen.
"Do you think I'm more pink or more white?"
Questioned a petal, unsure of her light.

The marigold chuckled, "You're both, my dear!
Depends on the angle and how much we cheer."
With a flick of her stem, she posed on a whim,
"Let's catch the wind and do a spin!"

Oh, they'd twirl and giggle, in playful delight,
As crickets provided a serenade nice.
Hummingbirds hovered, a flashy parade,
While blossoms bloomed boldly, not one was afraid.

So here's to reflections, silly and bright,
In the world made of blossoms that dance in moonlight.
With humor and charm, they flourish and fade,
In a garden of laughter, forever well-played.

Serene Reflections in Petal Pools

In a garden where laughter blooms,
Petals dance and share sweet tunes.
A bee flirts with a sly little wish,
While ants plot mischief, oh how delish!

The sun plays peek-a-boo with the grass,
Tickling daisies as they sass.
A ladybug dons a tiny cap,
Ready for a whimsical nap!

Lady in red with a bold, fat talk,
Stumbles about like a clumsy hawk.
While colors swirl in a playful spin,
Nature's jesters, let the fun begin!

Underneath skies, so vast and blue,
Petal puddles dream of a dew.
As the wind giggles, coaxing them near,
Even flowers join in with a cheer!

The Light Beneath the Velvet

In twilight's grip, where the petals sigh,
A glow flashes softly, oh my, oh my!
The blooms whisper secrets to the night,
As fireflies chase dreams in a delicate flight.

Beneath velvet skies, laughter can soar,
While daisies toss envy out the door.
A dandelion thinks he's a star on stage,
Prancing about, feeling like a sage!

What tales they weave, in colors bold,
Even the shy violets, tales untold.
Frolicsome evenings beg for a dance,
Jumbles and giggles in a sweet romance!

So pass the moonlight, let the shadows play,
In this garden of whimsy, come what may.
Laughter erupts in the cool of the night,
As petals bloom with sheer delight!

Portrait of Blossoms in Thought

Once a bloom sat in deep contemplation,
Crafting a tale of wild imagination.
With petals like pages, each turn revealed,
The humor of flora, never concealed.

A sunflower pondered the height of its peers,
While tulips recounted their youthful years.
But all of this deep thought turned quite farce,
As a clumsy wind knocked over a sparse!

They laughed at the clouds, all fluffy and bright,
For dodging the raindrops was quite a sight!
And in that moment, so free and merry,
A bug brought lunch, a picnic so cherry!

Thus blooms shade truths in their leafy caps,
With giggles and grins, no room for mishaps.
Portraits of laughter painted with glee,
In the garden where happiness runs free!

A Prism of Forgotten Scents

In the corner of the garden, scents collide,
Whispers of lavender take a wild ride.
The roses complain, 'We were fresh yesterday!'
Yet neglectful violets laugh and sway.

Hidden beneath heap, a daisy's lost charm,
But brings out the giggles with a wink and a harm.
'Who stole my perfume?' a petunia might shriek,
As the breeze carries tales both funky and sleek.

Orange zinnias sport a flamboyant hue,
With designs and laughter, they just love to do.
While marigolds sparkle, their jokes just so bright,
Petal confetti makes evening delight!

In this fragrant chaos, joy takes the lead,
Crafting a garden as odd as a breed.
For every last breath, a story to share,
In fragrant escapades, without a care!

Reflections in a Petal's Embrace

In a garden full of blooms, they sway,
Petals gossip, come out to play.
Each one thinks it's the life of the show,
While the daisies just roll their eyes, you know.

Bees carry tales from flower to flower,
While mice nibble cheese by the hour.
The tulips tango, the lilies laugh,
As the violets scribble their newest gaffe.

Sunshine tickles the petals bright,
Who knew flowers had such a byte?
They laugh in colors, a comical sight,
While planning their outfit for the night.

So let's sip tea with the blooms at play,
And hear what they chatter about all day.
In a floral world, where silliness reigns,
We'll dance with the petals, let go of our chains.

The Colors of Longing

In a painter's splash, colors collide,
The blues are giggling, the greens can't hide.
A funny mix, like socks on a cat,
Each hue whispers, 'Look, I can do that!'

Yellows are stealing the red's last bite,
While purples are planning a dance-off tonight.
There's laughter in every shade and tone,
As the browns sit grumpy, well, all alone.

Oh, how they long for a picnic spree,
Joined by the clouds, sipping on tea.
But while they dream under the sun so bright,
The colors clash, what a comical sight!

In this palette of dreams, relations unfold,
As paint drips down, a story retold.
So let's splash our worries, laugh at the mess,
And join in the colors, all in this jest.

Frayed Edges of Petal Dreams

Petals whisper secrets in corners unseen,
With edges frayed, they share what they mean.
A sunbeam tickles, and flowers all grin,
While making up stories where mischief begins.

The daffodils scheme with the nasturtiums bold,
While marigolds blink, thinking they're gold.
"Did you hear? The violets wore stripes today!"
"And the sunflowers claimed they could win a ballet!"

Every crease in their edges tells tales so sweet,
Of quests through the weeds and dances with feet.
In this wild garden, hilarity's found,
Where each petal's dream spins round and around.

And as they sway in the soft evening light,
These frayed little edges take flight in delight.
Join in the laughter and frolic with ease,
In the garden of dreams, let's sway like the breeze.

Magic in the Thorns

Beneath the thorns lies a trickster's grin,
Where flowers poke fun, let the games begin!
"Who needs a crown when you have these spikes?"
Said the cheeky blooms with their odd little bikes.

The thorns hold secrets, sharp but sly,
Ticklish whispers that flutter and fly.
While roses brag of their delicate style,
Thorns chuckle softly, "We've got the wild!"

Petals parade in their fanciest dress,
While thorns play pranks, life's little mess.
"What's a party without a jab or two?"
Said the prickle to the bloom in its dew.

So let the thorns weave their whimsical tales,
As petals float high on the gentle gales.
For in this garden, where laughter is born,
There's truly a magic found even in thorn.

Requiem for a Fallen Blossom

Once a flower full of cheer,
Now a snack for a hungry dear.
Flopping petals on the ground,
Shouting, "Hey, I'm stuck! Come 'round!"

Bees lament 'neath the blue sky,
Sipping nectar, oh so spry.
They miss the days of flamboyant flair,
Now it's just petals everywhere!

We gather 'round in floral haste,
"Who knew you'd make such a fine paste?"
Laughing branches sway in glee,
While ants plan their grand jubilee.

So here's to you, oh sprightly bloom,
Your giggles still lighten the room!
We'll dance upon your fallen kin,
With joy that lives where life begins.

Whispers of Color and Time

In the garden of silly schemes,
Colors clash like childhood dreams.
Yellow seems to woo the red,
While blue grumbles, "Get out of my bed!"

Time ticks wildly, petals fall,
The tulips start to host a ball.
Dancing roots in misfit shoes,
Making sure the soil gets views!

Sunlight sneaks a peek and giggles,
As daisies wiggle and do their wiggles.
"Who stepped on who?" they start to tease,
Pollen fights break in leafy breeze!

A color riot, a flamboyant quest,
Together they fail the growing test.
But laughter rings through their bright hues,
In a perfect mess of joyful news!

Portraits in Bloom's Embrace

There once was a flower named Sue,
Who painted herself a bright blue.
"Am I the sky?" she mused aloud,
While her friends giggled, feeling proud.

Marigolds argued, "We're the best!"
"But irises give quite the zest!"
They posed and preened for nature's lens,
Creating smiles that just won't end.

Sunflowers strike a sassy pose,
While peonies spill tales of woes.
"Why can't we all just get along?"
Because oftentimes, fun feels wrong!

But swirling colors know their place,
In the odd and quirky flower race.
Here's a portrait full of cheer,
A garden joke we all hold dear!

Fading Echoes Beneath the Bloom

Beneath the petals, gossip flows,
While dandelions plot their shows.
"Who came up with that silly dance?"
As bees rumble, "Give us a chance!"

Faded blooms play hide and seek,
Whispering secrets, a bit unique.
"Does this leaf make my butt look big?"
They giggle softly and do a jig.

Echoes of laughter fill the air,
With blossoms twirling, no hint of care.
In paths of green, where wild things roam,
They raise their voices, an uproarious home.

Fading echoes call out loud,
With petals flying, making crowds proud.
Let's toast to the laughter in bloom,
Where humor and flowers forever loom.

A Lament of Blooming Days

In the garden, blooms are spry,
But ask them, and they will sigh.
They'd love to dance, but have no feet,
Just sitting pretty in the heat.

The dandelions tease them so,
With wild hair and all aglow.
'Oh look at me!' they shout aloud,
While posies fuss beneath a cloud.

The bees just laugh and buzz around,
While petals plot upon the ground.
'Why do we bloom if not to brag?'
Yet all we feel is just a drag.

But when the rain begins to pour,
They laugh and say, 'We'll bloom once more!'
A cycle of joy and petal play,
In this wacky, wild blooming day!

The Dreamscape of Petals

In dreams, the petals take a flight,
Wearing pajamas, oh what a sight!
They twirl and swirl in moonlight's glow,
But woke up stiff, 'What a show!'

With sleepy heads and sleepy bees,
The daisies grumble with the breeze.
'We were dancing till dawn's first light!'
'Right,' says the tulip, 'You missed that fight.'

A poppy insists it's a fine ballet,
While thorns conspire to steal the day.
But laughter blooms where petals lie,
In dreamscape fun, they can't deny.

So heed this tale of floral jest,
While blooms may toil, they never rest.
For every giggle, every sprout,
Is nature's way to laugh out loud!

Echoing Colors of Dawn

At dawn, the colors kick and scream,
A sunrise tangled in a dream.
The orange laughs with rosy glee,
While violets gossip, 'Just let it be!'

The sunlight trips, a clumsy soul,
And colors merge in a joyful roll.
They paint the world in silly ways,
'Who knew? We'd shine through all the haze!'

But shadows lurk behind the trees,
Pretending they are just a tease.
'Why so bright?' the shadows pout,
'Can't a flower just chill out?'

Yet every hue starts laughing loud,
'Come on, gray! Join this colorful crowd!'
With echoes bright of every shade,
The dawn's delight can't be delayed!

A Garden's Secret Confessions

In the garden, secrets bloom,
With whispers soft, dispelling gloom.
The roses chuckle, 'What a mess!'
'We tangled stems, now look at us!'

The violets snicker, 'We're in a bind!'
While clovers tease, they're hard to find.
'What if we play hide and seek?'
'That sounds like fun!' they giggle and squeak.

Beneath the soil, worms boast and brag,
'Our digging skills are never a drag!'
While beetles wear their shiny suits,
Dancing around in their fancy boots.

So here's the scoop, as leaves afar,
In every bloom, there's a quirk or a star.
A garden's joy, with laughter rife,
Holds every secret, every life!

Senses Wrapped in Petal Dew

In morning light, they prance and sway,
Petals giggle, bright colors play.
Bees buzz past with a cheeky stare,
As ants do the cha-cha without a care.

Sniff this bloom, it's quite a tease,
A waft of laughter dances on the breeze.
Silly squirrels steal a fragrant taste,
While butterflies swirl, in joyful haste.

The daisies chuckle, their heads so high,
"Did you hear that joke?" they whisper and sigh.
A quip from a tulip, "Who knew this bliss?
Petalversations are quite hard to miss!"

So here we are, beneath the sun,
In a garden where giggles have just begun.
With scents that swirl and colors that cheer,
Life's a joke, and we're all in here!

The Poetry of Fragrant Secrets

A daffodil said, "I'm quite refined!"
"Where's your prose?" said the sweet lemon-lime.
"Blooming, blooming!" was the hopeful reply,
While lilacs whispered, "Let's give it a try!"

Rosemary laughed, sprigs tucked in tight,
"Who needs a sonnet when laughter's the light?"
With ruffles and puffs, the tulips took turns,
Reciting mad rhymes while the sun slowly burns.

Violets quipped, "We're delicate, yes,
But let's shake it up and cause some sweet mess!"
With pollen confetti thrown high in the air,
The garden erupted in colorful flair.

So join this dance, where scents blend and spin,
In the rhythm of petals, let the fun begin.
For in every whiff, and each tiny delight,
Lies a garden of laughter that blooms day and night!

Mosaics of Love in Bloom

In puddles of petals, love's colors collide,
With giggles from daisies that just won't subside.
"Oh, look at the tulips, all red with glee!"
"They're blushing," said pansies, "Just like you and me!"

Waltzing with wind, such romantic fun,
While chubby bees hum a love-filled run.
Starlit in gardens, oh what a show,
With scents that say, "Come on, let's go!"

"Who needs a valentine when blooms do the trick?"
The irises chuckled, "Here's a little pick!"
With petals for kisses and vines for embrace,
Flirting in colors, we find our own space.

From sun-kissed mornings to moonlight's caress,
Our mosaic of love, nothing less, just the best.
In this tapestry bright, all feelings unspooled,
A patchwork of giggles, forever uncooled.

Echoes from the Garden's Heart

Whispers of petals and hearty laughter,
A chorus of colors, happily after.
Bumblebees chuckle, "Let's dance 'round the fern!"
While daisies declare, "It's our time to learn!"

The garden speaks softly, secrets unfurl,
As tulips spin tales, giving blooms a whirl.
"How tall can you grow?" a marigold boasts,
"A height that will surely earn me the most!"

Even the shadows are dancing today,
With lilies that twirl in a comical sway.
"Why so serious?" they tease with a grin,
"Life's just a joke, let the fun now begin!"

So gather around for the show of delight,
In echoes of laughter, our spirits take flight.
For in this plot cozy, where petals do part,
We find all the joy from the garden's own heart!

Specks of Gold in Floral Grief

In a garden where daisies dance,
Petals giggle, a frolicsome prance.
The sunbeam shines on a clumsy bee,
Who tripped on a leaf, oh what a spree!

A lily chuckles, 'I'm feeling bold!'
While a dandelion leaks weed-sung gold.
They gossip softly, oh what a tune,
In the breeze, like a merry cartoon.

Pansies giggle at a crooked stem,
Wishing they had a dapper hem.
With pollen suits, they strut and boast,
In this flower patch, they're proud as toast!

But amid the laughter, petals may cry,
For morning dew drops make them sigh.
Yet, with each giggle and sunny glance,
They bring life to the garden's wild dance.

Crossroad of Petals and Time

At the intersection where blooms collide,
Daisies chat, their chatter won't hide.
A poppy slips, with a wink and blunder,
'Careful now, don't pit our wonder!'

Sunflowers argue over who's the tallest,
While marigolds claim they are the smartest.
'Grow up!' they shout, in a floral debate,
While a bug nearby just can't relate.

Lilies sigh from their quiet perch,
While violets fight for the best research.
'Who wears the crown of the garden flare?'
They giggle and squabble, oh, what a scare!

But time ticks on, with each passing day,
Changing their hues in a vibrant play.
For laughter and thorns twist together,
In this whimsical world of floral tether.

In the Shade of Thorns

Beneath the thorns, a rose basks bold,
Telling secrets of battles retold.
'You think you're tough, but I've been pricked!'
The petals laugh, 'We're too quick!'

The sun hugs softly, tickling bright,
While shadows dance in the moonlight.
Thorns make life tricky, it's secure,
Yet petals summon laughter pure.

'Careful, dear blooms, of the bumblebee!'
One hapless tulip is caught with glee.
Pollen clouds make them dance with flair,
While thorns just sit, a cautious pair.

So here's to the blooms, so bold and bright,
Joking with thorns, their sweet delight.
In the garden of giggles, love unfurls,
Even the prickliest can have a twirl.

Silent Serenade of Blossoms

In hushed tones, a petal shared,
'Why is the breeze so unprepared?'
With a quick wink, they hum a tune,
For flowers chat under the sly moon.

Daffodils sway with a cheeky grin,
Teasing the tulips, 'Come join in!'
While violets whisper their lilac spell,
In a chorus that rings like a bell.

The moonlight tickles the garden fair,
As blossoms blush without a care.
'We bloom and fade, but laugh along!'
In this floral world, they all belong.

So here's to the giggles in the night,
Where every petal finds delight.
In silence they sing, a joyous rhapsody,
In a garden that blooms with pure comicality!

Hues of Love in Silent Nights

In gardens where the flowers boast,
Their colors bright, they cook and toast.
A pink one whispers, 'I'm the best!'
While yellow giggles, 'I'd jest!'

They dance at night, a fragrant show,
With petals swaying to and fro.
The daisies tease the roses bold,
'Your stories, please, we've heard retold!'

They link their stems, a funny crew,
Who knew that blooms could crack a view?
Each bloom is dressed in vibrant glee,
With pollen jokes, they bring us glee!

Oh, laughter lingers in the air,
As blooms compete without a care.
In silent nights, they'll take their chance,
To tickle hearts with flower dance!

Gentle Touch of Blooming Time

In morning light, the petals peep,
They stretch and yawn from cozy sleep.
The lilac claims, 'I'm oh so sweet!'
While violets hum a rising beat.

They gossip 'neath the sunny rays,
About the blooms and wacky ways.
'I sprouted first,' a tulip claimed,
And now it seems he's very famed!

The daisies laugh, their heads do nod,
'Your fame's like pollen, just a fraud!'
With swaying stems and blooms so bright,
They plot a prank beneath the light.

Oh blooming time, with gentle touch,
Each petal's punchline means so much.
In nature's scheme, great fun is found,
With blooms who joke and dance around!

A Symphonic Garden of Longing

In symphonic blooms, a concert starts,
With buzzing bees and fluttering hearts.
The roses croon their sweetest tune,
While tulips sway beneath the moon.

Each blossom plays their unique part,
With laughter blooming in each heart.
The garden holds its breath in bliss,
As petals share a giggling kiss.

They tease the breeze, a playful chat,
'The daisies think they're where it's at!'
A symphony of color blares,
As blooms tell jokes no one compares.

In every corner, laughter's found,
As nature's music wraps around.
Oh, sing with me, dear blossom fair,
In this garden, we're a funny pair!

Nostalgia in Petal Form

In whispers soft, the petals sigh,
'Remember when we all got high?'
With fragrant tales of days gone past,
The blooms unite, their humor vast.

They gather 'round in summer's glow,
Recounting tales of winds that blow.
The peonies burst, 'I once got stuck,'
While foxgloves laugh, 'Now that's real luck!'

With colors bright and smiles galore,
They reignite what came before.
Each petal tells a joke or two,
Reminding us of sunny view.

In nostalgia's charm, they find their role,
In laughter's thrall, they warm the soul.
Through petals soft and scents so warm,
A gathering blooms, a joyful swarm!

Enchanted by the Fade

Petals dropping with a flair,
Leaves are spinning through the air.
I waved goodbye to a bright bouquet,
It said, "Don't mourn me, I'm on holiday!"

Grew a mustache made of green,
Dancing where I've never been.
Roses giggle in soft hues,
Whispering secrets with dew in shoes.

Their fragrance hides beneath a laugh,
Nature's odd, evocative craft.
The garden gossips, what a scene,
Telling tales of what has been!

As hues depart and fade away,
I'll tell my friends they went to play.
Let's toast to petals on their quest,
Flirting with wind, unbothered, blessed!

Veils of Fragrance and Light

Sunshine dips in fragrant pools,
While bees dance like happy fools.
Petals prance in summer breeze,
Whispering jokes to tease the bees.

The daisies wear their summer hats,
Playing hide and seek with bats.
Tulips giggle in the sun,
Shouting, 'Blooming is all in fun!'

With every drop of morning dew,
A flower's secret rendezvous.
They tell quite silly tales of old,
About dirt that turned to gold!

Veils of scents swirl in delight,
Each floral giggle, sheer delight.
Come join the fun, oh what a sight,
In the garden's playful light!

The Heartbeat of Nature

Nature's pulse, a playful beat,
Where petals jump around in heat.
The daisies throw a lively bash,
While thorns plot how to crash the stash!

Crickets chirp in rhythm grand,
Throwing beats across the land.
Flowers sway with silly grace,
Threading laughter through their lace.

Every bloom has jokes to share,
With bumble bees all unaware.
They buzz around, proclaiming cheer,
"Get on board, we're blooming here!"

Nature chuckles, don't you see?
It's a party filled with glee.
With every laugh, it's plain to note,
Life's a garden, that's the quote!

In the Shade of Blooming Memories

Under blooms that shade the day,
Old memories like flowers play.
Laughing buds in colors bright,
Whisper stories, pure delight.

A daffodil's mischievous grin,
Telling tales of where we've been.
Petals chatter, it's quite the scene,
Past adventures, lush and green.

Laughing lilies shake their heads,
Reminiscing on comfy beds.
Each blooming face remembers well,
The antics spun within their shell.

In fragrant shade we gather near,
Sharing giggles, bound by cheer.
Memories bloom beneath the sun,
In flowery fun, we've already won!

In the Shadow of Fragile Beauty

In the garden where blooms compete,
A daisy slips on its own feet.
It laughs so hard it starts to sway,
While sunflowers just snooze away.

A bee buzzes by with a grin,
Sipping sweet nectar, the dance begins.
But oh, that clumsy little bug,
Got tangled up in a big red rug!

Petals gossip in the bright sun's ray,
They whisper tales of the bees' ballet.
With tickles from the morning dew,
They chuckle at the chaos too!

So in this patch, forget your woes,
Join the laughter where the wild wind blows.
In every bloom, there's joy to find,
Like well-kept secrets, left behind.

Memories Carved in Petal Softness

Once I met a bloom so fair,
With petals soft like fluffy hair.
But every time the wind would toss,
It flipped and flopped—oh, what a loss!

The violets snickered, oh so sly,
As tulips tried to reach the sky.
Each time they stretched, they slipped and flailed,
In petal fights, few prevailed!

"Oh no! Watch out for that big bee!
He's got a taste for a flower spree!"
But the bloom just giggled, brave and bold,
Says, "I'm sweet, he's just a mold!"

So here we share, these silly blooms,
Creating joy, dispelling glooms.
In every color, pranks abound,
Memories in softness, laughter found.

The Dance of Scented Time

Tick tock, the petals sway,
In rhythm with the breeze today.
A funky dance beneath the sun,
With flowers twirling just for fun!

A daffodil spins, then trips on air,
The lilac giggles without a care.
In this bouquet of joyous cheers,
They dance away all worldly fears!

"Oh dear, look! That bud's a clown!
Keeps falling down, it wears a frown!"
But soon it joins the jolly crew,
With flips and flops, they start anew!

So as the sun dips, the moon takes chase,
These blooms will keep their lively pace.
The dance of scents will always rhyme,
In every petal, the joy of time!

Crimson Echoes on the Water

Beneath the bridge where ripples play,
A splash of red floats by today.
A petal giggles as it glides,
While fish below just hide in pride!

"I see you, fish! Don't be so shy,
We know you're just a finsy spy!"
The lily pads join in the joke,
While frogs croak loudly, like a folk.

The sun dips low, the shadows loom,
Reflections dance, they're in full bloom.
With each gentle wave, a burst of glee,
Nature's comedy for all to see!

So here among the crimson flows,
Laughter swells with every pose.
Echoes of fun on water bright,
In this garden, everything's light!

Petals in the Mirror

In the garden, I stand so tall,
Admiring my reflection, quite the ball.
But the petals giggle, sway with glee,
'We bloom for the bees, not the likes of thee.'

I tried a pose, with flair so grand,
Yet a squirrel nearby had a different plan.
He scurried and danced, all with a cheer,
'You think you're the star? Oh, bless your veneer!'

The sun shone bright with a wink and a grin,
While wildflowers chuckled at my chagrin.
'You've got the moves, but we have the sway,
In the dance of the wind, you can't lead the day!'

So I twirled around, in blossoms and mirth,
A show for the critters; this was my worth.
Yet the petals just giggled and rolled on the grass,
'You're a lovely human, but dear, please pass!'

Echoes of Crimson Blooms

Crimson blooms called to a fanciful dance,
While I stumbled in, thinking I'd prance.
The daisies laughed, saying, 'Not quite your scene,'
'You tread like a penguin, all awkward and keen!'

With petals like trumpets, they announced my blight,
'Oh human, dear friend, try to get it right!
Your rhythm's a riddle, a puzzling tune,
But at least you got style, like a late afternoon!'

I joined in their laughter, twirling on ground,
Each step was a giggle, each hop made a sound.
The bugs started clapping, the sun gave a cheer,
'Breathe deep the absurdity, hold it all near!'

In echoes of crimson, I found a new stride,
So I danced with the blooms, with joy as my guide.
For in gardens of folly, who needs an old rule?
Let laughter be planted; absurdity's cool!

Fragments of a Floral Dream

In a dream made of petals, I lost my way,
Chasing flowers that giggled, as they swayed and played.
The lilies took selfies, the violets grinned,
While I tripped and flew, a tumble to spin!

'Oh dear,' said the tulips, 'you dance like a fool!'
'Your moves are like puddles, in nobody's pool.'
But I just kept chuckling, through laughter and blooms,
Brushing off petals that dissolved all my glooms.

In fragments of floral, I stumbled and weaved,
Every misstep a memory, none should be grieved.
For a dandelion winked, with seeds blowing wide,
'This whimsical ballet, you've got nothing to hide!'

So round and round, through my dreams, I spun,
Each petal's a laugh, oh what silly fun!
Let the flowers remind me, with petals they gleam,
That life is a dance, in this floral dream!

Whispers Among Thorned Shadows

In the shadows of thorns, a commotion unfolds,
Where laughter and whispers make secrets untold.
Roses with thorns wave their playful pranks,
While I tread their kingdom, just giving my thanks.

A daisy chimed in, 'You've got guts, I will say,
To waltz through the thorns, you must like the fray!'
I chuckled and nodded, all masked by the green,
'Just here for the punchline, if you know what I mean!'

The blooms had a jest, with petals so bright,
'These thorns are just props, for a laugh in the night!'
With every poke and jab, I wiggled and danced,
'Who needs a safe space when laughter's enhanced?'

In whispers of shadows, we plotted our fun,
As petals erupted, like giggles unspun.
They're thorny, but funny, a fabulous scene,
In the garden of humor, where all can glean!

Blooming Soliloquies under Starry Skies

Under the stars, a flower spoke,
A petal's laugh, a thorn's old joke.
It twirled and danced, quite full of glee,
Saying, 'Watch out! Don't trip on me!'

With every bloom, confessions grew,
Of bees that flew and lovers too.
"I'm not just pretty," it said with flair,
"But do remind them, I also bear!"

In whispers soft, the buds conspired,
To spill the tea, like they were hired.
"Did you hear what Rosie said at noon?"
"No, what? Tell me more—was it a swoon?"

Laughter echoed through the night,
As petals giggled, oh what a sight!
Blooming secrets under skies so bright,
Nature's comedy, pure delight.

Glimpses of Lost Floral Dreams

Once in a field, dreams took flight,
A daisy sighed, 'I miss my height!'
A tulip chimed in, 'I once was grand—'
'Oh please,' said the lily, 'do take my hand!'

Each night they'd gather, a floral crew,
Wishing on stars and planning a stew.
"Let's cook up memories, a broth so dear,"
"Maybe a garden where we disappear!"

Thoughts of wild dances under the sun,
But rumors of weeds just weren't much fun.
"I'm not afraid!" the daisy would boast,
"Until they showed up, then I'd ghost!"

Time passed gently, as petals turned gray,
But laughter remained, come what may.
In dreams they frolicked, in moonlight's beam,
A silly parade of lost floral dreams.

The Tenderness of Thorns

In a garden bright, thorns hatched a plan,
To tickle the nose of a curious man.
"Let's dress up fancy in our sharp attire,"
They laughed and joked, a thorny choir!

A rose nearby rolled her lovely eyes,
"You won't get far with your prickly guise!"
"We'll charm him sweet, like sugar and spice,"
"Then watch him flee, thinking twice!"

The petals chimed in with whimsical cheer,
"Who needs defense when the world is near?"
But as the laughter filled up the air,
A bee buzzed past, and felt despair!

The irony struck as thorns stood tall,
With all their whims, they'd still take a fall.
But in this garden, laughter reborn,
They found tenderness, within their thorn.

Quiet Reverie of Petal Dreams

In a hush of night, when the moon grins wide,
A petal dreams of a carnival ride.
"Round and round, let's twirl and leap!"
"But tread with care, or we might weep!"

They planned grand feasts with dew drops fine,
While ants debated how to best align.
"I say a buffet of nature's delight!"
"Meh, that might lead to a midnight fight!"

In these sweet dreams, laughter took flight,
As petals whispered their deepest plight.
"If butterflies come, let them be bold!"
"But bring a snack, or we'll lose the gold!"

So here they rested, wrapped in their schemes,
O'er the quiet reverie of petal dreams.
They giggled, they plotted, and danced till dawn,
What fun it is to greet the morn!

www.ingramcontent.com/pod-product-compliance
Lightning Source LLC
Chambersburg PA
CBHW071844160426
43209CB00003B/406